w. e. smith

collected poems

1990 - 2025

Also by W. E. Smith

Novels

Tanaki on the Shore
Ver Sacrum, or "Heaven Help Us All"
Bal Harbour
I've Got a Right to Sing the Blues
And in the End: A Novel for Beatles Fans
Wolftamer (for middle grade)
Tanaki on the Move

Short Fiction

I Wanna Hear It Again
He on Honeydew Hath Fed

primitive encounters . . .

Fear

I have dreamt deeply, and am drunk with my dreams,
I do not want sleep, but only wings!
To fly over the night like a great swan or heron.

Poetry is wine-warm on my lips, and
the seed of all things, living and inanimate,
is in my song—if I sing,

And if I do not quaver, and quake, and quail,
at the approach of the Great White Light!

Invocation

But of what shall I sing?
Of life that needs no bounds?
Of eclipses, or of stars that burn
So brightly, from so far away, that light
I see tonight began before man was?

Follow me and, by the grace of gods, I will
Lead you near the source of things;
Do not fear, my hounds and I are known hereabouts,
We have hunted this wood many a season;
The castle is not far off . . .

Canticle

It is another day, another death,
And not a small death, but a great, full death,
Like the one we all fear and desire, and
It is midsummer and we still live
In the old brick buildings at the edge
Of the great and powerful Republic.

There is a mimosa up the way,
And at least a dozen rose bushes,
Whose branches were so overladen this warm
Spring, they arched to the ground bearing
Their pregnant weight of beauty and scent,
And two hydrangeas whose flowers are
Of holy blues, and violets and pinks,
And many other blessed things besides.

And if I can make this my canticle,
my Sacred music . . .
Perhaps this summer will not slip away
Like so many filaments of smoke,
Like so many others as I approach my
Two score years on this planet.

to the city

i will struggle with you again,
wrestle in sweat and tears, though
i know i will be defeated.

your concrete and steel are too much for me,
for my flesh, for saliva and hair.

but allow me a space, however small,
where i can feel victorious (if but a moment)
feel the sun on my face,
be cooled by the wind, hear the waters
falling, rushing,
converse with the starts, howl
toward the moon, scream in rage,
cackle hilariously,
with abandon spew my juices
over your still solidity.

This year's tardy spring

the night came on like a tiger
swallowing everything whole

the wind was up:
the seed pods we called helicopters
swept through the air in happy squadrons

a sun titanium struck the trees
in the middle of a rain storm;
electric drops danced in the sun-charged air

smaller pods and fuzzy
blew into the bath through the open window

a crow banked against the updraft
and settled surreptitiously in a pine

the thunderheads moved off to the east
pulling a frightful blue in their train

a robin sat on the iron rail
singing.

Let us absolve the days

Let us absolve the days
of all their leaky faucets
and rusty pipes,
of all the bad moods
and "Happy Birthdays!"
of tragedies large and small,
and so many things
too numerous to mention.

Let us allow
for a little misunderstanding
here and there.
Let us buy a pound
and pay for two,
walk a mile
because the buses aren't running;
keep our feet on the ground
though the world's beauty
stings like a lash.

Let us absolve the days,
especially
when they are tricked out
in all their finery,
with scarlet flowers,
gold-green birds,
and the river beyond.

Let us love one another
and not look down,
because the abyss
can make you dizzy,
and the lengthening shadows
call to an emptiness
that should not exist.

Morning

The day is young!
Housefront board blanched with morning
        luminescence,
Piece of weathered wood on the road: I pick it up,
Hold it in my hand, feel its holiness, walk on.
All is green, green is everything; this stand of sedge,
How quickly they've grown—surely they were not
So tall last week. A beetle on the pavement,
Cartouche of copper green; your outer-space head
So tender, crawl on my hand, find rough going
Through field of forearm hair, buzz flustered
And land on stalky blades—a forest of lawn.

Healing echinacea,
Ivy on a wall,
Cat scratching its ear,
Dove on a wire:
A day sums up the year.

Alright

If every street could be this street
and every twilight this twilight,

If every rain could be this rain
and every aroma this aroma,

If every chair could be this chair
and every waiter this waiter,

Every breeze this breeze,
every puddle these puddles,

I would be alright.

Lucky

I walk upon this giving Earth
Wishing to find my fellow beings
I don't know what their dangers are
How can I experience their pain their hope?
It seems I cannot know them
      in their totality
I suffer
      from this separation
I suffer
      from this not-knowing

Once the river came to me, in all its dark innocence
Bringing with it sediments and fishes
      swamp and current
      dragonfly and eagle
Like a mother it soothed me
Enfolding me like bread dough upon itself
—the cliffs spoke from the far bank
Enraged and flattered by my attention
Nothing seemed real
      except myself

The time will come for my own, lone journey
The day will break like white phosphorous
And something will begin to crumble
Somehow the people will know
Somehow the people will feel
Their knowledge of the ocean will come back to them
      suddenly, without warning
Shells, brine, seaweed and fishing boats
Will come into fashion
Will be à la mode.

Gulls

I must worship my own nameless gods
and suffer my own private hells;
My gods require no libations,
only every breath, step, word
My hells are like shackles and thorns—
too insignificant to mention.

Thousands of gulls gathered
on the Tidal Basin half-frozen,
Like the hopeful gaze of Jefferson,
basalt and gigantic, columned in
Greece; ever still.

They pecked at the open carcasses—
slashes of red in fish-brown—
Shouted triumphant over a prize:
others floated in the floes, belly up.

Fractured sun glittered on the surface,
a V of geese passed soundless,
disappeared over Hains Point,
A jet came roaring out of National,
drowning the silence
of a thousand shrill echoes.

I wish to straighten my body.
I wish to sum up all experience.
And, one day, I wish to die.

everyone's going faster
I go slower
everyone's getting more done
I get less done
people want efficiency
I think about life!
our children, sitting in cafés,
don't know why
the world is so absurd,
don't understand why
traffic is rushing past;
people with mortgages, plans,
bank accounts
mean nothing to them;
they listen to the music
on the radio,
careful not to go beyond
the cautiously perceived territory
of their more ennobling dreams,
—still attached, as it were,
to the umbilical of the heart
running backwards, past their births
connecting them to an unknown
but deeply familiar region;

One day they will come to the brink
and they will decide, inevitably,
that to live in this world
requires a price
(a mutual forgetting)
and they will rush past cafés
where their children sit,
listening to the music,
oblivious to their dilemmas
and their pains.

Europe

Transparent blue,
Tragic hour of evening!
The air is cooling, and
Lambent sun lies against the restaurants on Del Ray.

Standing outside the Bombay House, about to enter,
I look south and wish I were in Europe
—something red in the blood—
A tribal memory, the northern shores from which
Frisian hulls were launched against Camelot.

. . . streets paved with stones, and people in whose
Faces is reflected the history of the race,
Gabled roofs in the canals of Amsterdam.

With the remaining years of my life
I will live like a flame that will not die,
And speak not in language, but in mountains
And clouds, and my footfalls will not be heard
In city streets, but with leonine tread
I will range a Serengeti of the mind—
Roar noisily at an horizon that seems infinity,
Indistinct in the afternoon haze.

Another Spring

The dead colors of another spring:
I have not seen them,
Only dark blood
That flows through ancient channels,
Final promise of atonement
Through one act of pure grace.
Plastic colored eggs hung across
The face of a hedgerow cheer me
(Odd emblem of a painful death).
The crippled man, whom I daily greet,
Approaching on the road,
Old white station wagon droning past,
Birds!

time for a change

strangers mistake me for others
clasp my hand
pat me on the back;
I don't mind
maybe they know something
I don't!
something in the wind—
the scent of . . .
cherry blossoms by the river?
spring is here
it's time for a change.

If one could . . .

If one could truly comprehend
everything that makes up just one day:
a morning, night, a lazy afternoon,
constellations, coffees, smiles and sand,
hours, shoes, buses, candy . . .
If one could only comprehend . . .
then just one day
would be our entire and only epic,
would be our one god and true religion,
our journey and our destination.

If one could only comprehend
everything that makes up just one face,
a smile would be assigned
the mass of several galaxies,
eyes would be worshipped
like the deep, dark pools
where ancient Olmecs tossed
their lives' possessions;
noses would be conquered
by brave men wearing snowshoes,
leaning into the wind.

If one could truly comprehend
the power of just one love,
(my love for you)
an outstretched hand
would contain every answer
(and every question)
a touch would launch the pride
of infinitely powered vessels,
and the loving gods,
with so little to do,
would lie down for a long, long nap.

Aulis revisited

My heart is awake.
And to know so suddenly I am not one,
But part of One.

The clippings smelled of hay, and
Set me thinking of the old stable,
Where we mucked the stalls,
And piled high with hay, and bags of feed,
Commander Dirson's flatbed truck,
With the brothers Blair, two Homeric heroes
Who lost their way in the wings of history,
And wandered onto the stage of this strange century;
My brother Henry was our Agamemnon.

We hosed the aisles to keep down the dust,
Gave to each its ration of pellets and hay,
Teased the stable girls, and led horses out to
      pasture.

The sweaty flanks of a tired steed; the
Soaked flatness where saddle had been;
Hot breath felt through hide when you placed
A hand on the warm hollow of chest.

Ah, the smell of plunkards!
The old board and creosote!

I miss you . . . Iphigenia.

*and Pat could arc a bale into the loft with one
        groaning motion . . .*

There were two types of forks, the short ones,
with many tines, and the long, with
just four or five, more widely spaced.

The pickups crawled between the stalls,
we tossed the reeking fecundity into the back,
until each overflowed it gunwales,
leaving bits of wet straw and manure
        scattered in the aisle.

One had to be careful of certain horses—
a sudden flash from the sharp hooves of one of those
ancient plains rovers could lay you out.

We built fences and cleaned hooves with a tool
        made for the purpose.

We were young, and the world was our Apple.

It's hard to burrow into this world,
know it,
Who's who?
What's what?

I want my heart to be
stars . . .
bees . . .
If I could walk with a softer
—but broader,
step; somehow
incorporate streetcar bells
into custard pudding,
honey,
perhaps people would stop hiding
their names
under the soles
of shoes;
stop whispering
through strange conduits in
subterranean alleyways,
And perhaps
more than anything,
I, Bill Smith,
would learn to recognize
my own face
in the passing days.

A bird is a thing

A bird is a thing that flies,
tracing an arcing path across the glowing sky,
resting on trees, and fences, and wires,
and never lies down,
except to die.

A bird is light of body—
hold it in your hand,
as if nothing had happened,
an expanding space of tenderness,
makes itself felt
in the soul.

It has no face, but only eyes,
and a beak, which is—
mouth or nose?
how can you look into its soul,
when one eye looks here,
another on the other side?

A man is a thing that roams,
in search of seed
and something strong;
a bird is a man's eyes in the sky,
and never dies.

it was a summer evening
I walked,
feeling strained and moody;
birds of different colors
than I am wont to see
in the yard at the Friends school:
yellow finches and tanagers;
a woodpecker with
a dash of red
veered across the field
when I stopped to watch;
sky of aluminum blue
chalky cliffs of cloud
suddenly

time synced as . . .

a swallow dips madly before
ascending to a wire,
found myself drawn to the
park by vines of tiger lilies
hanging from bowers;
rounded three arborvitae
taller than I'd ever seen;
wondered I hadn't noticed them
before;

on their leeward side
filled my lungs with evergreen
walked through arbors;
leaving the park
encountered blooming
solitary yellow lily
beside the library.

why is heaven so far?

with autumn coming on
I listen to a set of Bill Evans'
(too many words are still unspoken)

the trees respond weakly to a sun
that bears ever toward the south
crepe myrtle blooms, like dried coral,
wrenched too soon from salt sea and life

songbirds are fewer
I see neither cardinal, nor jay
the dove sits not on the wire
squirrels busy burying nuts

rosebushes have been cut back
one or two right to the ground
it seems too cruel a cut
for this mellow season
already pregnant with melancholy and loss

orphic Bill flies into infinity
notes like gemstones
struck off an iceberg
scatter like swallows
in a Keatsian moment

mellow fruitfulness I know is at the core
—then why my agitation?
India is coming back
smell of temples and vermilion
shepherds in the road

this music has a way of taking me
forward and backward
I wonder who I am,
find myself in a moving middle
unable to call out

care must not be taken
the way is brief; overcome
by some feeling, I stop
to collect a single, waxen petal
watercolor washed pink

answering an ancient call
I offer it at the base of one
of the cherry trees on Manning Drive;
the following morning
only a shred of pink, nothing more.

Summer

The summer has overflowed its banks,
Sated me with its burgeoning life:
That profusion of black-eyed Susans
By the walk at road's bend, was
Too much; the cloying sweetness of scent
Made me turn and hurry on;
The crepe myrtle by the post office, too,
Covered with pink cones of coral,
I could not fix my gaze, my eyes
Sought the sidewalk, the street, anything
Without color—and this insane heat!
I have learned to enjoy reading accounts
Of Antarctic exploration,
And the search for the Northwest Passage,
And when Hudson's ship is locked in ice,
I congratulate the crew and envy them.

Strangers

There are strangers living in my house,
Many strangers—I don't know their names,
They come and go: silently, unnoticed,
Like so many Jean Valjeans; perhaps
I should ask them to leave, question
Their furtiveness; but they've been here so long,
So many years, I don't know where to begin.
When I encounter them in the hallway,
Some dark, stormy night, I turn quietly
And walk away, as if I had seen nothing,
Return to my room and stand by the window,
Mumbling softly to myself as with shaky hands
I attempt to light a candle in the rising wind.

If you are lucky . . .

And one day
if you are lucky
while walking in the fields
in a resplendent sun
the world will go
suddenly silent
like a mother, nursing

You will notice that
the grass is greener
than grass can be
the sky blue
and without clouds

You know you must
walk down the path
and into the woods
beside the creek;
crouching on its bank
you remember two deer
you once saw here

The stream throws off
a shimmering shield
of glorious light; giving
thanks you will rise,
continuing on the path
where the creek goes straight

You notice you have not
seen person, dog, nor bird
and feel happiness
knowing you have come
to an end with
nothing new to begin.

One day

one day,
just one small day
is all it takes;
and the universe comes down
the flowers bloom
babies cry
ditches are dug
(men wearing plastic hats)
the market is closed
traffic goes by
music sweet jazz plays
in the café
where I sit
a universe of dreams
in my hands
the girl explains
a caramel drink
to the clientele
shades of night go by
though it is yet morning
the day wraps itself up
(wraps around itself)
finishes as it begins
(begins while it is ending)
satisfaction inheres in things;
why struggle?

Spring—early

in February the rains came
also warm, sunny days
cardinals played through the thickets
the river churned a dance,
the "boy" blew hot and cold
across the Pacific
storms in battle order
waited to march upon
the California coast
hurricanes and tornadoes
blew over the South
the president tried to explain
the girl in the black beret
spoke of sending death and misery
against a brown desert people
—no one cared
Esmé stayed away
I held my breath.

Insomnia

It was that hour, night
or morning, when slippery slugs
ooze wet on the walk.

Overcome by breeze, I walk,
walk.

Traffic lights flash through the town, electricity
and colored glass.

Things look different at this hour:
glow-white flowers behind a wrought iron fence;
streetcorner mailboxes, like mute sentries
(reassuring reminders that the Republic stands)
dark recesses where old garages lurk.

Up ahead, the old kirk; Sunday morning soon,
people of the town will bring their heavy load
of sin to be
expiated,
purged,
expunged, and they
cleansed.

I will not be here, though I am not sinless.

In a shallow pool, reminder of yesterday's rain,
the oaks on the grounds of the Friends school;
George Fox: none of your sect ever
burned
anyone
for disagreeing.

God bless you all!

I wish to lay down the law.
I wish to straighten my body.
I wish to sum up all experience.
And, one day, I wish to die.

The leaves are swept

The leaves are swept
The leaves are blown
But my dear gods,
You have not flown.

The time is ripe
The season changing,
On earth's dark face
Wild winds are ranging.

The colored lights
Of red and green
Take me toward
A power unseen.

Poetry

The icy trees
A frozen night
Another smoke
To stem the fright

A woman gone
Life in arrears
Unspoken songs
Across the years

A lovely view
A different room
Yet still I feel
A certain gloom

But poetry mine
You mean the more
The further I'm cast
From the shore.

everyone is entitled to live in this world
to live life
to experience the migrations
of their dreams;
the man in the unlikely beret
a top-coated woman with briefcase
—the guy in shades,
they all know what they want,
and how to get it!
don't stand in their way!
don't impede them!
(I implore you)
caskets there are and plenty
for those who wish to stanch
the human spirit;
let us be in the light
let us be in the world
let us go into the meadows
where the sun shines
on the endless hills of
my unending youth.

Will the world come around?

Will the world come around?
Can I find my way?
When all is given,
Does anything remain?
Sunlight on the sidewalk,
The dark smell of coffee,
My steps on the earth,
Steady and ongoing.
Matter meeting time.
I see myself
Splayed out and tortured
Amid schedules and contracts,
Speeches and forebodings,
Steady within, knowing.
To embrace all, is all:
The man in the workboots,
The fat lady at the counter,
The driver of the truck,
The people speaking Spanish.
Where is the revolution?
When can all be?
Ejecting myself from myself,
Finding quiet, empty.
Embracing all,
Knowing nothing.
Sunlight on the sidewalk,
The dark smell of coffee,
Will the world come around?

I somber on

Trance-fed, I somber on
Only stalks have meaning
Stalks of lost mothers
Galloping over lighted fields
Liquid trust in knowing nothing.
Something seething,
Tranquil,
Fast epidermic and hydroid.
Calling out for names
That die in the wind,
Wasted words over such a brown country—
Over such a brown death.

I haven't been here long:
Only chasms have opened
To claim my dreams—
          lying dreams;
Fast, dwindling stars in teeming skies,
Liquid trucks on remorseless journeys,
Crossing some "other"
          to arrive at nowhere:
Like a cathedral in the small town,
English stone, and steps on a trodden path.
Bill.
Graves behind a wall.
Stone.
You can see nothing?
Forest.
Whites of witches eyes.

Drowning, hymns in my nose,
my throat,
Father take me down,
Further:
Cast on ahead . . .
What would be my preoccupations
If I were to sleep couched down
On some lotus reed?
Eternity is nothing to my eyes.
Something fabulous, extrinsic,
Concerning no one,
However small, however weak.
Can Gilberto sing?
You bet he can—and so could Brel.
Fabulous singers of fettered oceans,
Light rays on toward sunset.

The Omen

Starlings flocked in the holly-hedge
The Salvation Army bell tinkled over the intersection
        near the supermarket
Gray and white pigeons stood gallant on the wires,
The trees along the avenue
        were strung with glittering lights
I was satiated on Chinese fare
  —a crispness in the air
  —the rush hour traffic
Starlings began to leave the hedge,
Determined, fixedly, in numbers almost endless—
        too abundant for that simple space of green
By twos, by tens, they take flight, to join
Hundreds of kindred souls already
        winging, soaring, shuttling
In thickly woven formations over the traffic,
        the video store and the parking lot;
The driver of the tractor-trailer, who delivers
Cars to the automobile dealer,
Readies his rig, now empty for the journey
        Home;
It is growing dark

I step, my own homeward trek , along the sidewalk,
Something swoops—it is improbable,
I cannot at first take it in,
Coming from behind, low over my head,
A large brown hawk, its trajectory sure,
Clutches a glossed starling, jerking and frantic
        in its talons;
It rushes on ahead, rises to a bare limb
Behind the crab house,
Stands upon the still-clutched starling,
        —its prize;
The seafood man stands beside his truck,
His cart loaded with steaming boxes,
I look on in horror,
The feathers come first, pecked,
Scatter and float earthward through the branches,
I've seen the raptor around,
        for three weeks or more,
Then came the breast, the pecking
        more emphatic,
I know the viscera will be next;
I cannot watch, and hurry along;
Turning back, one last time,
The hawk gorges itself in the dying light.

Storm

The day is full, and I know
I can accept this—now.

The enchantress of another shore
Would teach me the hard names of things.

The breeze is playful now,
The leafy branches lift and sway,
Fall, lift and sway . . .

But soon it will turn violent,
Coarse, and great rivers of pure, sweet rain
Will call down the sidewalk,

Chasing a wind that gusts through my body
As through the timbered frame of a house half-built.

Sunday morning

Hurry and catch the day!
Before that old fart Cronus steal in
To trounce the illusions of May,
We live and breath for only an instant
—one silly instant.

And they've cut the stalks of the day lilies,
A battered baseball sits on the wall,
A squirrel pursues another 'cross wire and bough.

Dare I steal into the drive to better see
That great cedar that towers across the lawn?
A bunny sits wall-eyed watching me.

The lawn is yellow dry,
A swing hangs idle on a branch,
The woman's walking club comes by, relentless
Steppers, and the stalwart of the season,
Hydrangea, yet blooms.

Sunday morning.

we must carry on
—we of the human race
though conspiracies of Darkness
camp across the earth
with their diagrams and methods
their wheels and questions;
a new body has come upon me
I am not the same;
ships set sail
for distant ports
engines set in motion
progressions beyond even
your wild dreams!
but we carry on
walk upon the earth
with the sun shining
surely, we must walk
in darkness—the soil
with its grace, will
humble us, will
feed us, will
placate us
will capture us when
hearts, desperate of an answer
descend into a longing
too deep for memory
to contain.

Death

I discovered this morning that I was dead.
And what's worse, they'd already buried
"The body"—note the delicacy of phrase.
I set to thinking how I might dig it up,
What tools I might use: shovel, pick,
Iron bar to wedge under the coffin,
Crow bar to pry open the lid.
Pictured myself a Hamlet, contemplating
My own skull beside the yawning pit,
Thought of Lazarus, and what Jesus is reputed
To have said, about the dead burying the dead.

A worm is no less a thing than I,
We're each allotted a chit of life,
Before resolving again to clay, and
Across the eons, my three score and ten
Against his several months, who's counting?
And the incongruity of the thing,
Leads me to suppose there must be
something more than this "I."
I will be a man, because I know how to be a man.
If I knew how to be a worm, perhaps I'd be a worm.

I returned home today by different streets,
And made my peace with the cheery trees
On Manning Drive.

driving out bradley boulevard

late summers' evening air
wild kiss on the side of my face
the savagery of the human heart
is not mine—not mine

I can blast, I can blow
(winter cries)
and let me just tell you
the sky looked like an endgame—
the same foreboding,
without terror,
but only a logic
that
i have loved
and cherished.

we will see

I have sunken

I have sunken so far
into this American earth
I cannot move,
I will not move!
I have seen the highways, with their
toll plazas and interchanges,
service stations on shining plateaus,
seaports and burial grounds . . .
but I will not move—
not now!
I have only one day to live,
and I will stay sunken here
in my good, brown American earth,
and feel the pulse of a thousand generations,
like a river flowing over the sky,
someone will come
to play the celestifugal cymbals,
a child will pull a red wagon,
clanking along some silent street,
a mother will call out,
a father will break his life
on the bitter wheel . . .
love will serve its hidden purposes,
secrets will be revealed
only to be cast forever away,
no longer powerful, sad
and dilapidated.

On his person

In the pockets of his jacket,
Two Medjool dates in a plastic bag,
Four vitamin tablets in a wad of foil.

A rucksack containing three books:
Neruda, Nemerov and Hamsun,
Tea bags and a half loaf of bread.

In the left breast pocket,
The cheap plastic billfold, souvenir
From the BritRail pass he carried
Over England in the fall, a few bills,
Credit cards, drivers license, library card,
Old receipts—
All the indicia of citizenship,
Of personhood.

In the right, an absence
where his pen should have been.

In his chest, a stone,
Across his face, a cataract,
In the skull a torch, glue
Running down the spine and into
The peritoneal cavity.

A life.

Dream

The ship sails on
The sailors have deserted their posts—
Fie upon them!
I wildly roam the deck
My double tied to the soaring mast
Ghostly silence over the churning sea
No one left to hear my songs
Of Conquest and War,
No one against whom
To test my arm in athletic contests . . .

In this lonely night-world I feel the weight
Of a Polyphemic eye upon me
Upon my drenched and barnacled ship
The Sea is green, but does it matter?
A dream of green, nothing more . . .

In that wilderness

I tore my clothes on thorns
Cut my feet on sharp mouths of stones
Stung by buzzing insects I walked on . . .
Scorched by sun
Chilled under the cold moon
Cannot remember finding the hairy dog
Or did he find me?
Curled around his shaggy warmth
Slept on hard ground
Eating seeds and berries—
Stony, waterless land
Gave up hope of returning home
Scratched flinty drawings on rock walls
Bellowed in canyons
To hear the hollow report
Of a living god
The dog died
—was eaten
Delirious for a time
Came to shallow-running water
Lashed a raft and launched . . .

Time

Can crepe myrtle be in bloom?
Has time worn out so many ragged days,
When Jupiter whispered to the moon
Across dark waves of night and space?

Crow on the lawn.
Dove on a wire.
The rose has lost its pink and shows
A field of sepal stars, a universe
That now expires.

Prelude/ Interlude

I have spent a great deal of time
struggling to return
to one very small
place

where I lived in the earth
with its soil
in the wind—
in the sweet rain
a tree
a frog
a flower
a bird

The vastness of that
ever-changing sky moved
not over me, but
through me

every incline was
for bicycle sprints (headlong)
every tree was for climbing
every stream for wading
dog for barking
frog for catching
horse for riding (bareback, of course)
every mother was for hugging
father for guiding
brother for struggling

My loves were for all to see
nor were my hatreds hidden
and when I fought
it was not to wound
but to kill

I learned not so much
to live in the world
as to live in spite of it
and I wonder what I have hoped
to gain.

Forty

Only one way I know this life
And that is by breathing through the skin
Open to the world on all sides,
Shades of memory blending:
Fleeting images of people I have known
Distant figures in a Chinese painting . . .

Cannot bring down a sense of reality
Disturbs my dream with ugly talons
Now walking on through dangerous parks
Birds and children laugh and play
Sinister reminders of innocence unredeemed . . .

Perhaps the sun will dry me
Shrivel in me all that is unnecessary
Leaving a sense of hollowness
A cardinal flitting in the brush!

three occasional poems,
two visual poems,
haiku

I cried too[1]

O Prophetess! why have you abandoned us?
On what deep shore do you await the coming dawn,
Will you not sing a song, or two,
To ease the pain of memory?

I found you once, somewhere strange and new
You opened up to me, a world of heart and soul
Day by day the thought lingers, like wind chimes
Drifting in the evening. Where? Where?

You sang of rivers and Chinese restaurants, finally
You brought dew and flowers, and melancholy,
Your body was a holy flowing Madonna-image
Your robes touched the ground lightly where you
        walked,

We picnicked, and panicked; you fought on
Against the ignorance and the blindness,
The torpor of a world gone dead in the soul
And yet you lived, and spoke, and danced, and peace.

In what New York morning does your phantom
        linger?
On what hillside can I find you? Tell me
Now one of your more woeful tales, only lightly,
A light for me in a world made darker by your leaving.

Cover me with your mantel of grace, O Lady,
Saraswati One, bear your image truly now,
Give us comfort in your absence
Send us homeward with a harmony and a smile.

---

1. Upon learning of the death of Laura Nyro, April 8, 1997

Epithalamium

In time, the lines
of lives entwined,
like threads of cloth
in your daddy's machines—
—machines to buy a feast
of dreams—
unwind.

And none of our schemes
can slow the drift
from dream to dream
or make even one thing
hold true to itself
(or our conceptions)
for even the most
infinitesimal
space of time.

But—standing there in brocaded
white you shone
happy in womanhood
newly won, a gleaming moon
you'd found your sun;
and speeding on before the dawn
happy charioteer I
to drive the nuptial coach
toward the appointed revelries.

Then, low in the western sky
round and full:
the lunar orb
to bless your bond
against such fools
as those who rhyme
that lines of lives entwined
like threads of cloth
unwind
in time.

*On learning of the death of Carlos
Casteneda, from my friend Bob,
while visiting in California*

The valley spoke in doubtful pinks,
I sought a friend and river-wise,
Remembered what a mountain meant,
(wildcat death at shouldered heights),
Though nothing changed in a new-washed world,
A tale was told of a warrior's prize,
By a sapphire lake volcanoes rose,
(prescient words of ash and fire),
The waters moved their tireless wail,
And swallows lost themselves in flight.

Sycamore

I appreciate your spreading virtue,
Diaphanous green waving over morningtide mist;
Bless the ground with parasails fixed, yet free.
Mottled, dappled, you shed tough outer bark
As you grow, until smooth seal skin wraps you
Here and there visible, to the touch complete,
Continuous: I wish I had your virtue,
To cast off rough asperities as I grow,
And of all the trees whose ways I have on
My walks admired—oak, magnolia, cedar
And pine, some who aspire to heights celestial
(I think to organize a tree festival!)
None speak to me like your simple, spreading
                    Virtue
                    Virtue
                    Virtue
                    Virtue
                    Virtue
                    Virtue
                    Virtue
                    Virtue

I love a river.
  I will not name it,
    Because that would bring to mind
     lines on a map,
       Or a mere collection of water,
        And I know a river
          Is not a collection of water,
            Nor lines on a map,
              But has a living soul, and is a great
              Teacher of men;
            No wonder I exhale a sigh,
           When I breathe its vast expanse
         Between the shores of Rachel and Leah.

     Driving over the bridge one morning,
   Towards the great and solemn cemetery
    Where the nation's dead lie resting,
      I look over the rail toward Georgetown,
        Sculls with their outriggers
          Pass underneath on the misty surface,
           Like skimmers that darted so lightly
          Over marshy creeks, distant kin of this
        Mother of waters, where Eric Jones and I stalked
      Sleek, muscular bullfrogs, hunters by instinct . . .

The river offers never the same face,
  But is sometimes turgid, brown, sometimes
 Slate, calm, or brilliant
Blue, sparkling, joyous and radiant,
It reflects clouds, trees, buildings,
And my moods;
  But always the river flows, and as
   Cars lurch frantically over rush-hour bridges
    The river knows, she knows.

a flight of herons
winging over river rocks
in the steady rain

Alberta burning—
sparrow feeds her fledgling chick,
in the rainy yard

disappearing act—
overcast obscures the range,
where is Yonah Mountain!

like a flight of birds
cherry leaves, autumn gold
in the morning sky

driving home at dusk
on the hillsides, mimosas,
bursting out like flame

purple irises
how high they lift their petals!
north wind blowing cold

morning Tokyo sky
clouds of presence indistinct
pilgrim trail awaits!

torii in the sea
deep as heart's lost yearning
Tanabe evening falls

knowing I must die
I seek an ancient wisdom
kami's clear, bright way

from Earth's deep heart
Yunomine's healing waters—
Hongu Taisha calls

travels . . .

home and abroad

Two young Americans tour the Continent
(1976)

I turn a seeking face to the world,
I speak with whispered voice;
We made for Montreal in June,
A service station plaza quivered in the evening light,
Upstate New York grass was green,
—the road was wide,
No one knew us, and we were young.

Brautigan and Vonnegut in our minds,
Loggins, Taylor in our ears,
The world was wild, we wilder still,
The praeries stretched on endlessly,
Mollifying Boston's uproar,
—we flowed under the impetus
Of Niagara's tumultous torrent.

Cornfields and cornfields, night baseball
In some small town, where were we?
Campgrounds and campgrounds, cold showers
And a tarpaulin on the ground,
Doubled back, lean-to like, clasped
In the doors of a '74 Chevrolet,
A row of logs holding the crease.

The slaughter yards were rank and bitter,
The Dakotas wide and long,
Black Hills and Badlands sucked us deeper
Into America, as into some eddying pool;
We drove through a majesty of sky until,
Far in the distance, surrounded in haze,
The Rockies came into view . . .

We rose and rose, climbed and climbed
Through gargantuan worlds—Ponderosa pine,
And always that sky, that sky . . .
In Yellowstone meadows we stalked elk,
Lifted obsidian from hallowed cliffs,
Drove the dusty roads of antelope—
Plains of buffalo and moose in the wood.

Brother mine, you enfolded me once
In your small arms, and taught me things
You learned at school, strange symbols
On a small green board in an upstairs room;
With brother Tim we slid down the hill
On our lunchboxes
When it was covered with ice.

West of the Rockies we waded
Into the vast Saltiness to see
If we could float, as we'd been told;
Traversed great bleached flats
Like the rocket cars we admired
In magazines you bought at the pharmacy
Under the dentist office.

Yellowstone's geysers erupting within,
Moose and antelope still in mind's eye,
We tried our luck in Reno,
And left none the richer;
At Yosemite hiked an alpine meadow
Above Halfdome, left the park
Alongside the sparkling stream.

Bob, we called you Tweety Bird
In Mister Walker's metal shop,
And laughed with glee insane,
When Harry McKivegan, old and gray,
Flustered with rage, took hold of you
By collar, and sent you mock-reeling
Into halls where Gann and I stool waiting.

No, you would be no Latin scholar,
But a scholar just the same,
(Under a spreading pine, by the Seven Eleven
You passed the hollow pipe of oblivion,
And laughed and coughed and spoke of peace);
In a Berkeley house you danced,
The Grateful Dead on the stereo.

Maine had not held you nor ivy walls,
And onto California you roamed and slept
In hills above Cal for a space of time
Before settling into a cozy house,
With two strong women of your tribe;
We left you to a western destiny,
And through the fog we headed south.

To cliffs where Miller watched the dawn
And wrote *Orange Blossoms of Hieronymous Bosch*;
In L.A. Hank found a high school flame;
We wondered at Japanese restaurants,
And film crews on the sidewalks
(My memory hazes like the rusty sky
Over the freeway to Anaheim.)

So that is life?
We saw what we did and moved on.
(Goddess, I knew not of your deeper strains,
Sorrow, fulfillment and reeds in the wind)
But we talked into the night,
And matched our wits against a world
That seemed to bring us history's march.

Covered with the tarpaulin we slept,
Youth sandwich on the ground,
Tarpaulin aboave, tarpaulin below,
And drove across a desert,
One hundred fourteen in the shade,
And miles upon miles the Navajo Nation,
A lonely gas station and fences.

Mother you bore three sons and a girl,
Seeds in the wind, seeds in the wind,
Two sons in a '74 Chevy somewhere
West of the Mississippi, east of the coast,
On a mesa top in the desert,
Astonished at clay ovens and a church
Built by conquistadors.

The bats poured out of Carlsbad's mouth,
Trying to tell the world
Something of night, and of the hunt;
"It is a world of night," they sang,
"It is a world of flight," we heard,
And into Texas we road and the Alamo:
And Abe said we never should have fought.

Mother you bore two sons and a girl,
Seeds in the wind, seeds in the wind;
Two seeds east of the Mississippi,
West of the coast: caverns, geysers, women,
Mountains, meadows, cities, buffalo,
All behind us now, a feeling of strangeness—
In the pit of the stomach, something New.

Something New has happened Now, forget
The past, wear a new face, face
The world, snakes and alligators,
A snake trapper who scared the living
Shite out of me in the lavatory
Of a north Florida campground,
Where mosquitoes plagued our sleep.

With beady eyes and smile deranged,
He showed me his blade, how sharp, how sharp;
We packed up and left at three a.m.,
The mosquitoes, snake hunter, and
Alligators, plashing in the canal,
Had their victory; we were on the road,
With dawn breaking over the flat horizon.

And if I don't mention New Orleans
Honky-tonks, and queens in drag,
It is only because a mother
Bore three sons and a daughter, three
Sons and a daughter; seeds in the wind,
Yes in the wind, and I didn't know that Satchmo
Road a junk wagon, and played a tin horn.

India

people and their cows
India
dobi takes the laundry
India
darshan afternoons
India
sky of low clouds
India
water buffalo in the road
India
clamor in the marketplace
India
monkeys on the roof
India
temples revisited
India
song of the koyal
India
heart spinning like a wheel
India
ragas and rishis
India
soul burning like ice
India
vector undetermined
India.

Bombay

This is where the road stops,
India.
Even the birds look old,
ancient
City of vastness,
slums of the poor,
ripe fruits,
Taxi driver fearless as Vishnu
driving Arjuna's chariot.

South of Mysore

Saints and sinners,
all the same.
Day and night,
no different.
Motor scooters in the street
and sheep,
buses too—
all illusions.
Govinda too illusory.

Dobi's son

The dobi's son is dead,
A fever took him hence,
The rainy season starts,
A dobi's son is dead.

The dobi's son is dead,
The rainy season starts,
There'll be no wash today,
A dobi's son is dead.

A dobi's son is dead,
There'll be no wash today,
A mother mourns her child,
The dobi's son is dead.

The rainy season starts,
There'll be no wash today,
A mother mourns her child,
The dobi's son is dead.

Untitled Philadelphia

We all will come round to this place,
Where nothing is what it seems
And the wind blows in small, mournful gusts;
The people of the future will bow down
Before the gods of yesterday,
Hang their heads in prayer—ashamed
At all the tricks, the deceit and lies
            the treachery and confusion;
The Love of the great white angel of morning
Will spread over the pavements of the city,
People will come up from the underground
After waiting out storms of rage
            that blighted the days,
The dawn will break with a new Clean-ness
Some improbable sisters of mercy will
Capture a small, common rodent,
Only to set it free in the morning splendor.

Television, cars and computers
Will go crying to their cold, arid mother
        bitter and afraid;
Their legions will forsake them
To stand upon the shore rocks,
High above the breakers
And issue a prayer to fulfill the wind
        in all its promise;
Nothing will be the same—
Not even women will know what to do,
        or exactly who they are

But until that bright day
I will continue my search
Should it take me to Japan
        or Kalamazoo
And if I find a solitary bull
        red and magnificent
Standing mutely in a field in Portugal,
While an autumn sun plays lightly
Upon the still-green grass,
I will consider myself
        lucky.
        Amen.

perhaps . . .

if I am sad
perhaps—
it is because
there are no fires,
no goldfish,
no stars in my soup!
How many days must go by—
like this?
When will the snows come?
(surely a snowman will
cheer me);
Where are the poets
wearing berets
late into the night
in cafés;
speaking of love
singing
of sea and stars,
of little dogs,
Chinese horoscopes,
heliotropes and gaslamps?

Sometime,
I will take a trip
to Portugal but
not near the city
—though the sea is
beautiful; but the sun
splayed on open fields,
the laughter of children
in the wind
a horse-drawn cart,
subtle crimson dying light
waves of wheat
is what I have dreamt of
Perhaps—
sadness is not a thing
but an absence of things,
like your bright eyes
when I turn at the sound
of a phantom rustling
in the evening air.

A Prayer from the Cliffs of Sagres

Sacred earth, hear me,
We are only here for a brief hour
Before passing on to some other night,
Some other depth

When man's stature finally dissolves
Back into your placid waiting soil,
Is anything gained?
Is anything taken away?

The heart of the world-soul
Continues to beat,
Like the stars that shine
Without seeming relent,
Upon the ocean swells that surge
Against these hallowed cliffs.

Sacred Spirit, hear me,
Just one small speck
Confronting the grandeur of this sea,
Itself an inkling of the infinitude
That rings us round.

Give us eyes to see,
Give us organs to smell, hear,
Feel your presence—
Let us know in what direction
To set our course;
Give us an honest weathercock,
And true.

Come between us
And our fears and desires,
Our fantasies and what-ifs.
Let our days be filled with happy endings,
That are always beginning.

Speak to us in a whisper,
In a hushed presence
That is felt in the bones,
Like the waves below these cliffs,
The sand between my toes,
The lazy afternoon,
And a scruffy dog lying
On the sun-washed pavement.

Give us our Darkness,
And let us see that light
That incorporates the very blackness
Of our journey.

When we are gone
Let these waves still crash,
Let this sound still linger,
Let an afternoon follow a morning
Like the bells of an ice cream truck.

Speak to us in a hushed voice . . .
We do not hear well,
Let us know you are there,
But do not frighten us
With loud displays

I ask too much
And know too little
But keep you in mind.

from the

mountain . . .

what is sacred?

what is sacred?
it is people being together
it is the night sky
it is a hummingbird
it is water flowing
it is woman
it is man
it is stone, a leaf, and dirt
it is a baby crying
the night singing
katydids and frogs
it is a swamp
mucous and tears
it is blood
it is bone
arrows arcing
horses running
cows lowing
crackers and tea

A poem for winter

Unhinged from all destiny,
my backpath littered with
tattered remnants of broken selves,
derelict and discarded;
observant, with neither point of reference
nor goals to run to,
I stay upon the earth, waiting,
and see the seasons go by,
the atmosphere, the stars,
the flora and the fauna,
the comings and the goings;
I desire nothing,
but to live like a winter afternoon:
a silent room, still,
with gentle light,
nowhere to go,
nothing to do,
but to watch the slow procession,
never changing, and without drama
of any consequence,
of this endless world.

all one

to drift over this world
    like air
to float through my life
    like water
to know only molecules
    and space
to watch for nothing,
    wait for nothing
two yellow butterflies,
    a woodpecker
snails that cling to the curb
    in Little Havana
to take my fellow human beings
    by the sleeves of their garments
let them know we are one
    in pain
all one,
    in solitude

I was made from earth

I was made from earth,
fashioned by the wind,
raised by the sun,
nursed by forests,
watched over by the sky,
taught by clouds.

the fervent grass embraced me,
creeks and streams, they sang to me,
I fell in love with several flowers,
entered into solemn pacts with mongrel dogs,
held counsel with horses, and
heard, in the fields, an
always expanding symphony.

People around me seemed lost,
their eyes—great, blank shells—
could not see one another;
they stumbled, solitary and silent,
along the corridors of the world,
arms stretched out, offering gifts no
one could touch, no one accepted.

I took the matter up with the mongrel dogs,
held counsel with the horses,
asked several flowers what could be done;
the creeks, they sang to me and, in the fields,
I heard the magnificent symphony of time;
I went to my first tutors, the clouds,
but their answers drifted away on the wind.

one day I found myself lost,
my eyes great, blank shells,
unable to see my fellow human beings;
stumbling, solitary and silent,
I roamed the corridors of the world,
arms stretched out, offering gifts no
one could touch, no one accepted.

I could not find the mongrel dogs,
the horses had fled to Colorado,
tall buildings blocked the sun,
the wind was exiled to the plains,
I could not see the clouds;
"where are the streams and the creeks,"
I bellowed to passersby, "and the great
billowing symphonies of the fields?"
they introduced me to an engineer.

the creeks and streams, he told me,
fidgeting with a slide rule in his breast pocket,
had been banished underground;
they were disturbing, he said, the
automobiles and the buses;
the fields had become shopping malls.

I thanked him for his advice,
and finding a rusty, blind eye in the
skin of the earth, climbed through;
after a week of searching
I found a stream; it smelled funny,
but still it was singing.

I have lived here since that day,
listening to the singing creek;
odd Tuesdays I climb back to the surface,
lift the rusty blind eye and look about,
to see what is happening.

tall buildings block the sun,
the wind is exiled to the plains,
I cannot see the clouds;
the fields have become shopping malls;
the people seem lost,
their eyes, great, blank shells,
cannot see one another;
stumbling, solitary and silent,
along the corridors of the world,
arms stretched out, they offer gifts
no one can touch, no one accepts.

I slowly lower the big, rusty eye,
climb back to my place by the creek,
where I sit listening to its song,
thinking about my old friends, the mongrel dogs,
dreaming of horses and Colorado,
waiting to die.

and so we shared

I have known bright, sunny days
        I was so free!
The brown earth was my brother
        that's how it was!
On spreading lawns we played our games,
        and never cared!
The sun shone down on everyone
        and so we shared.

And glory come

No use speaking of rebuilding,
When there's nothing left to rebuild with,
In life you only get so many chances,
And this world is for the agile,
And this world is for the swift.

So lay down all your burdens,
And forget about tomorrow,
Forget about the past,
And lay aside your sorrow
And take up all your pieces,
And the things that you have borrowed,
And put them in a basket,
And bring them to the altar,
Of dreams that never happened,
And love that didn't ripen,
And peace that didn't come,
And words that were not spoken,
And children who die waiting
For the world to hear their cries,
And mothers with hearts breaking
When they gaze into their eyes,
And friends who never answered,
And poems left unwritten,
And journeys never taken,
And races never run.

But friends will be remembered,
And held in my embrace,
When of this world there's nothing left,
—Of my life, not a trace,
My brothers I will hold,
As when we were small boys,
My sister, parents, all the rest,
Though darkness come and nothingness,
And I be naught; yet light will shine,
And clouds will part,
And glory come.

alone

My isolation is exquisite;
weeks and years it has taken,
to learn to be so alone.

At first I knew communion;
the people who surrounded me,
seemed so much my flesh,
so much my heart,
their smiles, my smiles,
their tears, my tears
their wanderings, my wanderings,
their returnings, my returnings.

One day there was a great noise,
like dishes breaking,
everyone was scattered, shattered,
we did not grow apart,
it was more like we shrunk away,
their smiles and tears were no longer
my smiles and tears,
their wanderings and returnings,
not my wanderings, not my returnings.

We were all lost
in the sad airiness of the world;
making appointments,
checking off to-do lists,
watching characters on television
while we silently ruminated
about why we are here.

We were instructed
by the most proper officiants,
in what to think,
in what to say;
they led us in hearty choruses,
of slogans and learned analyses,
some more plausible than others,
like stones they emerged from our mouths,
—like stones.

I tried to ask the Beatles,
but they were otherwise occupied,
and it was only by some strange grace that,
one night, in the most small
hours of the morning,
finding myself in chambers of ice,
of melancholy and stardust,
I heard singing, and
jazzmen blowing horns,
and Bill Evans playing softly,
and knew again the warmth of the world.

In the morning, sunlight
streamed through the windows,
like ripe watermelon, like trumpets
blaring; but the soft catechism of my heart,
winding along, raveling back,
into the night just passed,
found only disconnected pieces;
flabbergasted and speechless
I read the news of a pitiless war;
superfluous and silent,
I wrote this poem,
that no one will read.

all I know is that
the gaily colored flags
snapped and furled
in the brusque April breeze
on their tall silver poles
in the mountain tourist town,
where the purling, curling
river, swollen with snow melt
ran fast and clear;
dark pink flowers
gracile and delicate
covered the loropetalum
that lined the courtyard
of the old German inn,
where forsythia bloomed
and cherry trees;
children smiled and
stroked the necks
of the big draft horses
hitched to the carriages
that stood beside
the little town square;
the great spring sun
shone madly through the
blustering wind;
the river, under the bridge
ran fast and clear;
outside of town
in the forests, great
clouds of blooming
dogwood, everywhere

among the things I like
—are coconut, mountains
snowmelt rushing through ditches
memories of cousins when we were small
hummingbirds, woodpeckers,
pickup trucks from the 1950s
Parcheesi and Chinese checkers
rodeos, the Beatles
Peter and Gordan, awnings
porch swings, England
San Miguel de Allende
Pablo Neruda, yoga, track meets
the ocean, sea shells,
tourism, amphibians, music
children, lady bugs and beetles
friendly dogs, driving caps
summer storms, spring rain
snow, lightning, the Chesapeake Bay
old men, writers
shamanism, the sun
the moon, stargazing
your soft eyes
your warm embrace
swimming pools, Bill Evans
the Dave Brubeck Quartet
playing the piano
my sister's laughter
pens
your soft eyes
your warm embrace
the quiet days
I spend here with you

catastrophe

catastrophe will come
catastrophe upon catastrophe
it is in the nature of things;
so do not despair
for the broken tooth
the sudden debt
the lover who is leaving
the car that will not start
plans that go awry;
the poetry of life
is always there,
it is not leaving
and does not know
about the tooth, the debt
the car, or your plans;
make a pact with life:
that you will always seek it
there, where poetry lives
—every day
in some essential way:
a tree, a child, a cloud;
though catastrophe come
—and it will—
that the broken things
not shroud your life
in doubt, in fear;

—that the mind
(freedom its best part)
be ever tuned
to the song of the world
underlying, ongoing,
its many colors
always changing,
infinitely varied, never wrong,
waiting, yielding, fertile;
that your life be strong,
as mud is strong,
as a chickadee is strong;
that, like water flowing
transparent, moving,
receptive, reflecting
every passing cloud,
trees and children,
your substance be
subtle, varied
light and dark
shallow and deep
honest, without
end or beginning

have you known the fullness of life?

have you known the fullness of life?
have you walked into the ocean
climbed a mountain
loved a woman

have you been to Mexico
looked into a crow's eye
ridden a horse;
have you tasted the desert,
its voluminous silence

have you cast the *I Ching*
walked a dog who licked your face,
cared for a child
driven a motorcycle

have you seen a line of horses
slowly rambling, timeless,
along a gully in the dry, brown earth
between San Miguel de Allende and Guanajuato

have you watched the stars
along about midnight,
seen the moon glaze the woods
with its silver sheen

have you been a friend
have you had your doubts
have you never wavered
have you always wavered

have you tried your best
have you broken down
have you seen the lawns, spread
green and lambent, a late summer's day

have you heard the Beatles
have you danced the twist
have you been to Oklahoma
—if only in your mind

have you seen the aged
slowly fading
held the hand
weak and hollow-boned

have you been yourself
have you tried to sing;
groped toward infinity
known the fullness of life?

small medicine

Heart-broken, fleeing a city
where tragic scenes unfolded
—structures in ruins;
those I loved most
drinking up grief
as it flowed from the taps;
I found myself in open country
desolate and alone, barren,
carrying my small medicine:
fleeing, and yet,
attempting to return

I met people there, women,
they tried to love me
in sudden groves, by running rivers
at sinister encampments
in softly colored dawns;
but soon they learned
one and all
that I was a phantom self
made of hunger and dread
the other still in the city
I had left behind me

Unable to feel
unable to stay
unable to see their eyes
I found work, simple,
with my hands
and played my guitar
and João Gilberto sang
and Gato Barbieri blew his sax
with passion so great you thought
the instrument would break

In time life became
more quiet; I wore a mask
and learned to pretend;
now they were happy
but still I could not see their eyes;
I went to the shaman priest
he burned pungent herbs
he sounded his drum,
in the lodge we went
and the heat, and the stones;
I saw his eyes,
there were others, too
in some new place,
their eyes, too, I saw

I began to return
the city was still there
but it had changed;
those I loved most
had also wandered
to other countries
other cities;
I think I saw their eyes
I do not know if they saw mine

Carrying my small medicine,
I struggle to make sense of it all,
I will travel no more
but stay where I have now returned
journeying in all directions
seeking poetry
in the changing winds;
watching Hawk
float over these woods,
abiding with my love;
from time to time
ringing a very quiet bell,
trying to do better

9 798991 312950